1

Functional Training for Tennis

The Sequel to the book
How the Tennis Gods Move

www.DanMcCain.com

Contents

Introduction

Image 1a. Seeing Roger's resurgence.

"My game is all about footwork," Roger Federer once said in a 2006 interview. "If I move well, I play well."

These words rang true more than ever when we saw this thirty-six year old father of four emerge out of a six month leave of absence from the tour with fresh, healthy legs and another chance to play. The Swiss Maestro remains among the best examples of how movement is connected to technique and style of play.

It's been painfully obvious over the past few years how Father Time imposed some injuries on the 20-time grand slam champion. His hampered movement affected his tactical decision-making.

The healthy Roger Federer we saw win the Australian Open and Wimbledon in 2017 displayed similar movement quality we saw in 2006. Soaring in confidence, his all-court game style, filled with variety, creativity, and plenty of net appearances, re-emerged.

While the book How the Tennis Gods Move focused on movement principles, it also began to explore concepts of training fundamentally sound movement in tennis. This book arms readers with a more diverse collection of functional training exercises that enable players to mimic the movement of the pros and maximize efficiency, precision and power on court.

Many people associate training exercises with fitness. Putting the time in to get into great aerobic and/or anaerobic shape. Feeling the burn. That is not what this book about. Not even close.

Mark Kovacs
@MKovacsPhD

Do not confuse activity and calories burned with athletic improvement. The easiest thing in the world is to make someone tired.

12/30/16, 3:14 PM

9 RETWEETS **21** LIKES

Image 1b. Screenshot from Mark Kovacs Twitter account.

In his article Footwork - The Bailey Method (Part One), footwork and tennis trainer David Bailey outlined five areas to address when analyzing movement - what he calls "the 5 R's."

①"Getting Ready by being up on your toes and then creating a strong foundation with your legs when the opponent strikes the ball.②Reading the opponent's approaching ball into a specific footwork zone on the court.③Reacting out to this ball with Out steps and setting up the feet into a hitting stance.④Responding with a contact move and its corresponding balance move. And, finally,⑤Recovering ideally to the mid point recovery position of your opponent's next shot."

11

"When you put the 5 R's together," he wrote, "you get a Completing of the Circle with your footwork, and this should happen time and time again with the hitting of every ball."

This book explores what Bailey's sentiments reflect and how to effectively train those concepts. This objective involves showing, through images, the integration of movement and technique of the pros - and how it all can be developed effectively through functional training.

The ebook version of this work contains short videos (often accompanied by voiceover) that put a wide range of functional training methods on display. Nearly every image sequence shown throughout these pages come alive in video format in the ebook.

Android and iPhone users can download the Amazon Kindle app for free and view the ebook through the app once it's been purchased.

Image 1c.

The functional training exercises from the methodology these pages unfold can achieve a range of objectives. When performed well, they mimic ideal movement and mechanics we see from top ATP and WTA pros, isolate specific skills and enhance habit building. They can be used with players of a variety ages and ability levels either during dynamic warm ups prior to practices or matches, or within progressions during lessons and clinics.

Many of these exercises are performed without a racquet or a ball. By taking the shot out of the equation, players can place their focus entirely on skill development.

Often players lose sight of skill acquisition during practices when their focus shifts toward results, making or missing shots, and winning or losing points. With no shot, there is no distraction.

The functional training tools used here include Bosu balls, medicine balls, hoola hoops, fitness sticks, fitness steps and step ladders. Using these tools provide a unique visual and kinesthetic addition to how players normally train. This gives players a greater than usual opportunity to build sound habits, or what North American culture refers to as "muscle memory."

When we practice, our brain sends a signal down our nervous system to instruct our bodies what to do. The more we practice, the more robust these signals become.

Our brain produces a chemical called myelin, which "is a sausage-shaped layer of dense fat that wraps around the nerve fibers," according to Daniel Coyle in his New York Times article *How to Grow A Super Athlete*.

"Myelin works the same way that rubber insulation works on a wire, keeping the signal strong by preventing electrical impulses from leaking out...The little sausages of myelin get thicker when the nerve is repeatedly stimulated. The thicker the myelin gets, the better it insulates and the faster and more accurately the signals travel."

By coaching players verbally through these functional training exercises, players are stimulated in multiple different ways compared to normal practice. These exercises empower players to build ideal habits through enhanced visual, kinesthetic, and auditory learning. Optimizing this mind-body connection can advance a player's movement pattern awareness.

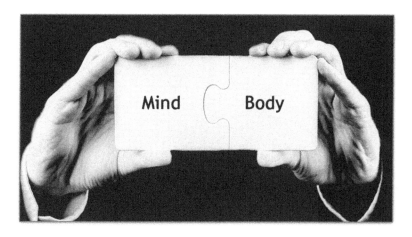

Image 1d.

Chapter 1. Movement Principles: An Overview

Image 1d.

Before training to become a better mover on court, we must know what to train and why. Building good habits requires a genuine understanding of what needs to be developed and why.

"Tennis needs a common, shared model for teaching technique & movement," wrote former ATP World #7 Tim Mayotte in a 2017 blog post on Universal Tennis. He's absolutely right.

First developed by the LTA, the ITF published the BIOMEC Model to coaches in 1995. According to the ITF book *Biomechanics of Advanced Tennis*, the BIOMEC acronym serves as a "method to educate coaches in tennis biomechanics and allow them to better integrate it into their on-court coaching."

- B - Balance
- I - Inertia
- O - Opposite Forces (GRF)
- M - Momentum
- E - Elastic Energy
- C - Coordination (Kinetic) Chain

This outline of movement fundamentals summarizes how the tennis gods move, serving as a guide that integrates movement and racquet technique. It provides players and coaches a foundation for how we all can become more fluid, efficient, explosive and more confident players.

The BIOMEC Model also provides concepts that feed into a more specific system of evaluating mechanics to be explored in the following pages. This more specific system involves the ideal sequences of things. By defining the specific stages the tennis gods use on each stroke, coaches and players can effectively train movement and mechanics.

Sound movement fundamentals provide a range of benefits for players at all levels. These benefits include dynamic balance, effortless power, enhanced endurance, fluid shotmaking, and efficient preparation and thus maximum time to receive their opponents' shots and respond.

As a result, sound movement on court leads to increased confidence for top pros, more options with shot selection emerge, and thus a greater ability to discover and execute strategies. The consistency of movement fundamentals predict the consistency of shotmaking. Images 1e - 1k show an overview of the movement patterns of Federer and Djokovic. Both players receive nearly identical situations and display nearly identical movement patterns.

Split Step - Unit Turn / Toes Pivot - Crossover Step

Image 1e.

Image 1h.

Image 1i.

While the BIOMEC Method provides insight into movement fundamentals as a whole, the method Tim Mayotte uses, as we will see, builds from these concepts and provides a more useful, more specific method for players and coaches to utilize.

It has to do with mapping out the sequence of things.

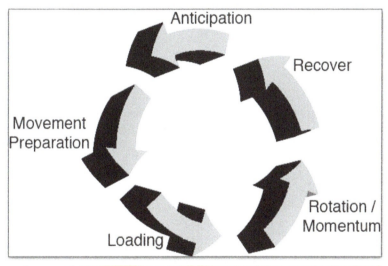

Image 1j. *An Overview of the Sequential Stages of a Stroke*

Chapter 2. Where The Sequence Starts

Image 2a. The Sequence of Kim Clisters' slice backhand.

When the tennis gods move, they do things in a particular order. Analyzing and executing the sequence of things in the right order can make a huge difference for any player in their preparation, timing, effort loads, fluidity, and more.

Knowing the ideal sequence helps players understand and value preparation. It empowers them to fully utilize the forces of the human body in motion. It helps coaches correct the cause of mechanical breakdowns rather than the symptoms. It enables them to instruct the player's body in motion with simple and effective messages.

The first thing the tennis gods do on every shot is often considered by many to be one of those difficult to describe intangibles that smart players "just know how to do."   In reality, this skill can be described, detailed and developed like other skills in the game.

Anyone with a growth mindset knows that skills, abilities and characteristics can be developed. So can this one.

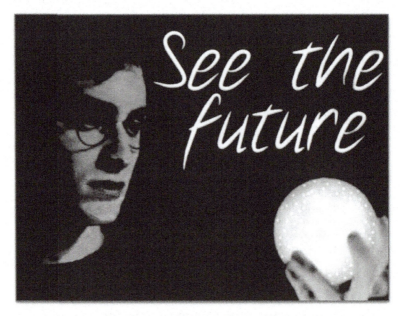

Image 2b: Happy Potter looks into a crystal ball.

Anticipation is often chalked up by many players and coaches as some kind of genetic gift that some people simply have or do not have. It affects court sense, a player's intuition, shot selection, judgement and overall movement.

Anticipation has much to do with memory and perception. Knowing the opponent impacts how one can predict an opponent's behavior. In The Art of War, Sun Tzu famously wrote "Know thy self, know thy enemy. A thousand battles, a thousand victories."

Opponent body types, past and present mental states and match situations all influence anticipation. Mentally logging technical proficiency in certain areas, tactical patterns and past decision-making factor into learning opponents' preferences, tendencies and general ability in various aspects of the game.

Aspects of the environment also influence anticipation for high performance players. The wind, temperature, and even size of the court (outside the lines) regularly affect individual comfort zones. Awareness of how the court surface affects the height and speed of the bounce - and how it affects a specific opponent - can also have a dramatic affect on judgement and decision-making.

While this may sound like a lot for one person to absorb, the human brain has more than enough computing power to process all this information as it accumulates. Our brains work far better than any supercomputer ever yet invented.

We have about one hundred billion brain cells. Our neurons can fire about two hundred times per second, with each neuron connected to about a thousand other neurons. Do the math on all that and we can make about twenty million billion calculations per second.

Chunking is a term referring to the process of taking individual pieces of information (chunks) and grouping them into larger units. We do this when we anticipate in order to read our opponents' shots so we can make instinctive decisions on when to move, where to move, how to set up for our shots and where to send them.

Because we can all process so much information so quickly, experienced players can have reliable anticipation under these relatively complex circumstances. Those who place attention on their opponents, various aspects of their games, and also maintain an awareness of the environment can develop good anticipation.

Image2c. Patrick Rafter on a defensive backhand.

Acronyms can make things memorable. Because we chunk information when we anticipate, using an acronym to chunk the information of how we anticipate seems appropriate.

The S.S.A.S acronym stands for reading:

- the Situation
- the Spin (Type)
- the Arc (Height and Trajectory)
- the (Racquet) Speed

According to the American Psychological Association, a growing body of research suggests that humor can "improve student performance by reducing anxiety, boosting participation and increasing students' motivation to focus on the material."

27

"Moreover," the APA continued, "the benefits might not be limited to students: Research suggests that students rate professors who make learning fun significantly higher than others."

When I spell sass wrong and students call me out on it, I tell them to stop being so sassy. And then I reiterate that anticipating should be the first thing they do on every shot.

Reading the situation is the most complex aspect of anticipation because it involves the environment (wind, temperature, court surface), opponent tendencies, mental state and body type. These factors surround the moment to moment subconscious anticipation high performance players use during points.

From one moment to the next, opponents are placed in various positions during points as they develop. By recognizing where an opponent is on the court, how much time he has and whether or not he makes contact in the strike zone, a player can gain a sense of what's about to happen.

This not only helps a player play the point in the present moment, it also can help you build adaptable strategies over time. Once a player's shot flies into the opponent's side of the court, he can notice if the opponent has been put into a relatively offensive, neutral or defensive situation.   By taking note of an opponent's degree of difficulty, one can predict how strong or weak the opponent's reply will likely be.

Here's a *T.I.P.* for remembering three specific criteria that, when combined,   make some shots easier or more difficult.

* *Time* (the amount of time an opponent has to set up for and respond to your shot)
* *Impact* (is your opponent's impact, or contact point in or out of his strike zone?)
* *Positioning* (where is your opponent's court positioning?)

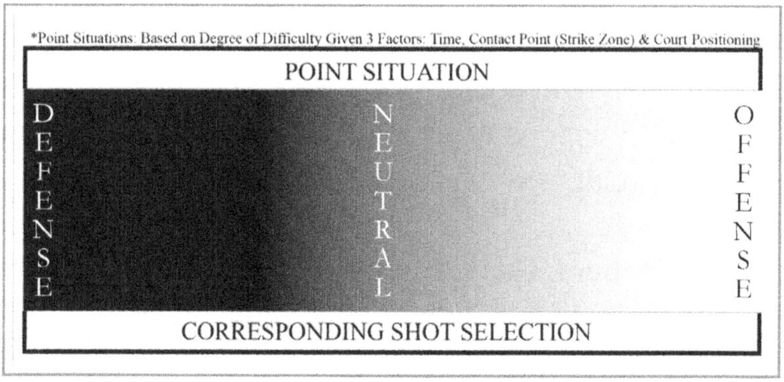

Image 2d. Point Situation ID chart.

Life is not black or fifty percent gray or totally white. Shades of gray exist. Point situations also function this way. They are not just offensive, neutral or defensive. They can part offensive and part neutral, or part neutral and part defensive. It's all about degree of difficulty for a player from one shot situation to the next.

Using anticipation contributes to a player's intuition. A smart player not only can recognize the degree of difficulty each shot within a point presents, he also uses that information to heavily influence his own shot selection.

On the other side of the net, a player with good anticipation skills recognizes his opponent's situation within a point and the degree of difficulty an opponent has on a particular shot. Identifying this in context with an opponent's shot selection tendencies can significantly contribute to a player's instinctual sense of how an opponent will respond in various scenarios within a point.

Richard Gasquet drives though an offensive backhand in Image 2e below. With plenty of time and excellent court positioning, he makes contact easily in his strike zone.

Image 2e.

In Image 2f, Djokovic prepares to hit a neutral backhand. Nadal reaches for a very defensive backhand in Image 2g.

Image 2f.

Image 2g.

In the middle of point play, developing anticipation has much to do with having a watchful eye. Looking for obvious technical cues is a big part of it. Identifying the grips, backswings, and racquet speed opponents use from one shot to another can serve as reliable predictors of shot speed, depth and spin types - all of which help players read the bounce.

Jo-Wilfried Tsonga's grip and backswing in Image 2h give us important information about the shot he is about to hit. His grip tells us the type of spin he wants to hit.   In this case, Tsonga prepares to drive his backhand with some amount of topspin.

The amount he drops his racquet head tells us how high he intends to hit his shot.   This gives us a sense of the trajectory and amount of arc he soon will send.

Image 2h. Tsonga prepares for a two-handed backhand.

Federer's grip and backswing in Image 2i clearly demonstrate he intends to slice this upcoming backhand.

Image 2i. Federer prepares for a slice backhand.

After identifying the point situation, grip and backswing, observing the racquet speed and swing shape through contact provides vital information about the amount of spin, direction and speed of an opponent's shot. This provides information on time available for preparation, the bounce of the opponent's shot, and where in the court one must move in order to set up to respond.

Image 2j. Federer accelerates through the hitting zone.

Observing these key moments in an opponent's preparation and swing shape provides more than just an instinctual sense of the impending shot type and quality during a point.   It enables players to more easily predict and read the bounce, as well as providing a natural sense of how to respond.

Perhaps the most profound benefit of consistent anticipation is the wealth of information that can be collected over time.   Tendencies of where opponent's like to send certain shots in certain situations become more predictable over time. Players who anticipate well begin to notice weaknesses in their opponents. One may recognize a particular opponent has a great backhand in general, but struggles on lower, shorter backhands.

One who anticipates well may recognize, for example, that despite the fact that his opponent's forehand is his biggest weapon, that forehand generally excels the most in the middle of the court and in his backhand corner (hitting inside-out forehands). One may notice that same player with the devastating forehand may actually be vulnerable when pulled wide to his forehand corner.

The Mirroring Drill is one on court exercise that I utilize with students during racquet warm ups, skill development drills, and also during games and point play to develop anticipation. In this rally-based exercise, the student must watch and receive the shot that I hit and then send back the same type of shot.

Image 2k.

For example, if, during the rally, I hit a slice groundstroke deep in the court, the student must follow suit and slice his groundstroke back to me. If I send a slower, loopy topspin shot crosscourt, she must send a slow, loopy crosscourt shot back. If I drive a shot hard and flat down the line, he must drive his shot back to me hard and flat down the line.

This Mirroring drill, which can also be implemented into point play, forces the student to observe their opponent's movement preparation, court positioning, racquet preparation and swing shape closely to be able to receive my shot comfortably and send an identical response back with quality.

Chapter 3. Movement Preparation

Image 3a. Federer's movement preparation.

The tennis gods begin their preparation with the following sequence:

1.   Anticipation
2.   Movement Preparation

In Image 3b below, Djokovic lands his split step. Upon landing, he pivots his feet and shifts his weight to his right, which then enables him to push off into a crossover step.

Image 3b: Djokovic's Movement Preparation.

By watching their opponents move to and swing through their shots, the pros not only know what type of shot to prepare for, they also know when to start preparing. If anticipation is like the keys to your car, then movement preparation is the ignition. Without turning the keys into the ignition, you can't start the car.

Sound movement preparation gives the top pros balance, time and a quick first step. Beginning as the opponent starts his forward swing toward the ball, ideal split steps make the body lighter and ready to spring in any direction.

The best movers in the game often land their split steps with relatively wide base and a specific foot sequence that enables them to turn and move quickly. ITPA founder Dr. Mark Kovacs discussed the nuances of the split step in his article Movement for Tennis: The Importance of Lateral Training, where he outlined what he called the gravity step.

Great anticipation often results in the split step, unit turn and crossover step performed in one seamless move - particularly in lateral movement situations. In the staggered split step shown in Image Sequence 3c, Djokovic lands his the foot furthest from the ball first.   As his foot closer to the ball lands second, his right foot and shin pivot to his right, like a door hinge opening up.   His center of gravity then shifts to his right, activating a light, quick crossover step.

Image Sequence 3d. Djokovic performs a gravity step.

Like every skill in tennis, movement preparation can be trained and practiced. Great movement preparation habits stem from productive practices that prioritize these elements that make up efficient movement to each shot.

"I find the best way to understand the contact moves is to feel them. Life is about experiencing not exhibiting," wrote footwork specialist David Bailey in his article about The Bailey Method.

"I am a huge fan of shadow tennis," Bailey continued, "which is where you practice all your moves without the ball, with or without the racquet, and on or off a tennis court. I believe it's essential to learn the contact moves in this way before you go on court using balls."

In the spirit of shadow tennis that Bailey praised, the following images outline functional training concepts for movement preparation. These exercises were designed to enable players to develop efficient movement over short distances and force them into effective movement patterns.

Image 3e.

These functional training shadow exercises involve players simply hopping off or jumping over things in order to manufacture the split step - unit turn - crossover step sequence.

Images 3e and 3f show a student of mine (Harrison Lee) using a fitness step to help him develop his movement preparation on his backhand. His objective is to hop off the fitness step (positioned parallel with the baseline) and use a gravity step before moving to his left for a shadow backhand.

Image 3f.

By repositioning the fitness step, a different set of functional training exercises can force players into performing a gravity step to begin the shadow stroke. In Images 3g and 3h below, a student (Alex Loope) begins behind the fitness step, which now is placed perpendicular from the baseline.

In the functional training exercise in Images 8g and 8h, his task is to move up to the fitness step and land only one of his feet on the fitness step. To force the staggered split step, he jumps up and lands his split step with his right foot on the fitness step first and his left foot on the ground second.

Image 3g.

During this exercise, Alex and I discussed how this exercise relates to a specific tactical situation. It mimics a point situation where, in a baseline rally, he had (on the previous shot) been pushed back deep in the court in his forehand corner.

Alex begins this exercise recovering back up to a neutral court position to begin his split step, at which point he sees his opponent send a shot to his backhand corner. Thus he starts well behind the fitness step and moves up to it to begin the shadow stroke.

Image 3g shows the initial action of his fitness step enabled gravity step. Image 3h shows the whole action of this functional training exercise.

Image 3h.

In Image 3i, Alex begins this shadow stroke using a typical fitness step exercise. This forces him to execute a gravity step before shadowing another backhand.

Image 3i.

Image 3j shows Alex using another common fitness step exercise to precede and facilitate the his movement preparation of this exercise. Instead of a shadow stroke, we use a medicine ball toss. While Images 3j and 3k show the initial action, Image 3l shows the whole action.

Image 3j.

Image 3k.

Image 8l.

Jumping over things can also help players train their movement preparation.

Image 3m.

In Images 3m, 3n and 3o, Vignesh Akkina jumps over a row of three medicine balls to activate his movement preparation.

Image 3n.

Image 3o.

Any tennis-specific fitness or functional training should contain zero potential risk for injuries and be age appropriate. Most of the exercises in this book do not involve a player hitting a shot. With no shot, no distraction of making or missing a shot occurs and full attention can be paid to the skill being developed.

Image 3p.

Targets are typically placed in areas in the court for players to aim their shots. Targets can also be used to direct movement. In images 3p and 3q, Harrison's first task is to initiate a split step, with his left foot landing in the hoola hoop to his left and his right foot landing in the hoola hoop to his right. His second task is to then make a crossover step with his left leg into the third hoola hoop furthest to his immediate right. The more reps he performs, the more a natural gravity step emerges.

Image 3q.

Image 3r.

Harrison's third task is to perform a shadow stroke forehand in this lateral movement situation. Specifically, he must load his right leg inside the hoola hoop near the singles sideline, execute an ideal shadow forehand stroke and finish with both legs outside the hoola hoop.

This functional training exercise helps Harrison build a wide range of sound movement and rotation habits. But our focus hones in on his movement preparation in this lesson.

Chapter 4. Loading and Elastic Energy

Image 4a. A student works on loading and momentum in a medicine ball exercise.

Elastic energy refers to the stretch and spring of major muscle groups, tendons, ligaments and fascia that provide us all with potential and kinetic energy. In Image 4b below, Juan Carlos Ferrero's forehand functions like a coiled spring.

With a comfortably wide base, he loads his body weight primarily onto his bent right leg into a semi-open stance. His shoulders turn further than his hips, stretching his trunk muscles and tissue, priming the rotation of his shoulders. The simultaneous loading of his upper and lower body maximizes the coil before springing into his shot.

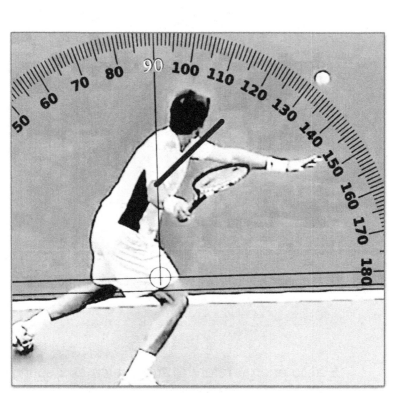

Image 4b. Juan Carlos Ferrero turning his shoulders approximately 120 degrees.

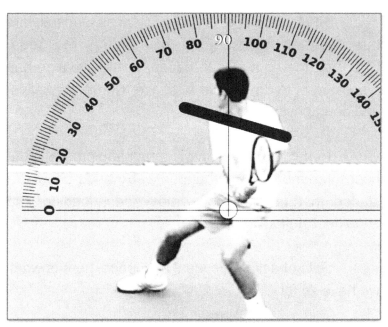

Image 4c. Djokovic loading on a closed stance backhand.

Loading also facilitates dynamic balance. When the tennis gods gain explosive momentum moving around the court to set up for their shots as quickly as possible, loading slows that momentum down a bit. This provides poise and enhanced vision between eyes and the ball.

Little adjustment steps are often necessary prior to setting up into a stance to load the legs. These little adjustment steps enable the pros to set up with an ideal amount of space between themselves and the ball.

Square, closed or open stances encapsulate the common terminology of loading the legs. Choosing the right stance based on the situation has a great deal to do with time, space, where the ball is, and court positioning.

To put it in more simple terms, the pros with the best forehand and two-handed backhands choose a stance that facilitates the most ideal loading and shoulder rotation.

Going back to the ideal sequence, here is what we have so far:

1.   Anticipate
2.   Split Step
3.   Turn (and pivot the toes)
4.   Run or Move (often beginning with a crossover step)
5.   Loading the Upper and Lower body (with a stance that facilitates ideal shoulder rotation)

The images below show some functional training concepts that help train players to access available elastic energy. The objective of these exercises is to load both the upper and lower body on forehands and backhands by putting the large muscle groups on stretch. The intent with loading the lower body is for the player to place the majority of his or her body weight onto one leg. Loading the upper body involves turning the line of the shoulders further than the hips.

Image 4d. Student Jed Bryan holds a 5 lb. fitness bar.

Image 4e.

In this exercise, Jed exaggerates the knee bend to load his outside leg while turning his shoulders further than his hips.   Because, in this particular lesson, we placed the primary technical focus on loading his outside leg, he intentionally executes a knee bend that puts him lower than necessary. Over time Jed's learning style consistently responded from different ways of exaggerating specific skills during functional training exercises or stationary hand feeding drills.

To make the next functional training exercise more natural, we began our progression with this common fitness step exercise shown in Image 4f.

Image 4f.

The exercises shown in Image 4g develops Jed's loading skills for his open stance forehand.

62

Image 4h shows how we worked on his open stance backhand.

Image 4g.

Image 4h.

Jed bought into this skill development progression upon realizing how the exercises and drills related to tactical scenarios within point play. Once he recognized that loading his outside leg benefitted him during lateral movement situations on his forehand and lateral movement situations with time pressure and a high bounce on his two-handed backhand, he became motivated.

Through these drills and some live hitting, he discovered loading his outside leg in these situations enhanced his dynamic balance, his ability to rotate his shoulders (and therefore improved his contact point). Images 4i and 4j introduce another functional training concept where we utilized the same 5 pound fitness bar as before and some hoola hoops.

Image 4i.

The objective of this exercise is to mimic an open stance forehand situation with forward momentum, either within a rally or on a return of serve.

Image 4j.

To execute this exercise, Jed has been instructed to load his right into an open stance behind one hoola hoop, then spring and rotate his shoulders and hips like would an ideal forehand. His left leg finishes inside the hoola hoop and his right leg finishes in front of the hoola hoop.

By lining up a number of hoola hoops in a row, Jed can move back behind the next hoola hoop for multiple reps. Images 4k and 4l illustrate the same exercise using a shadow stroke with the racquet.

Image 4k.

Image 4m.

Chapter 5. All Things Feed The King

Image 5a. Nadal.

While every player has unique strengths, weaknesses and needs, having a system in place that emphasizes specific technical areas can provide clarity. With a philosophy that arranges the technical aspects of a stroke into a hierarchy of priorities, players can more intimately understand ideal mechanics. Coaches can empower their students to refine movement and stroke production with simple, specific goals.

At our club in Virginia Beach, we have six clay courts and three full time coaches. This program has helped raise and train kids across every age group that have won state, national and international tournament titles. Many received college scholarships. Some have played futures and challengers on the pro tour.

Our club coaches operate with the same, simple coaching philosophy. This provides players consistent feedback as they move up and across the programs we offer, giving them a seamless playing experience.

At the club, we have all kinds of cue phrases. One that we frequently use is: "All things feed the king." This references our philosophy on biomechanics and technique.

The King? Shoulder Rotation.

While this discussion is limited to forehands and two-handed backhands, the phrase serves us all as a potent reminder of why we do all the things we do. It gives players motivation to execute the ideal sequence of things.

Image 5b.

Fundamentally sound shoulder rotation requires dynamic balance and linear momentum. It requires players to use anticipation and good movement preparation to give them enough time to fully rotate their shoulders on these shots. Sound shoulder rotation enables ideal contact points (which provides leverage with the arms and thus power), fluid follow throughs, efficient power generation, and significantly contributes to shot accuracy.

Image 5c. David Ferrer rotates his shoulders through an inside out forehand.

To ensure purposeful practices, players need to know what to train. Understanding the ideal amount of angular momentum on fundamentally sound forehands and two-handed backhands can give players a specific vision of how to operate. Because the line of the shoulders (beginning from one shoulder along the collar bone to the other shoulder) can turn and rotate further than the hips, the shoulders generate the most angular momentum within the torso.

It helps to recognize the different moments of shoulder rotation in relation to the swing path. Specific verbal cues can help make it simple. Being specific narrows the focus to task relevant cues. One way is to refer to the moment before and during the backswing as the "shoulder turn." This allows the angular momentum of the body rotation during the forward swing and finish to be referred to as the "shoulder rotation."

On his shoulder turn in Image 5d, the angle of the line of French Open champion Juan Carlos Ferrero's shoulders is approximately 120 degrees when he begins his backswing.

Image 5d. Former ATP #1 ranked Juan Carlos Ferrero's shoulder turn as he loads.

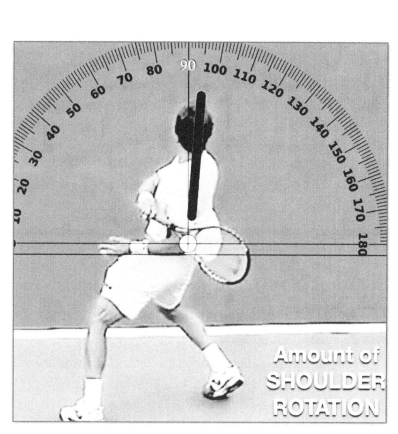

Image 5e. Ferrero's shoulder rotation.

In Image 5e, Ferrero rotates the line of his shoulders over 180 degrees on this forehand , just as Djokovic does on his backhand shown in Images 5f and 5g.

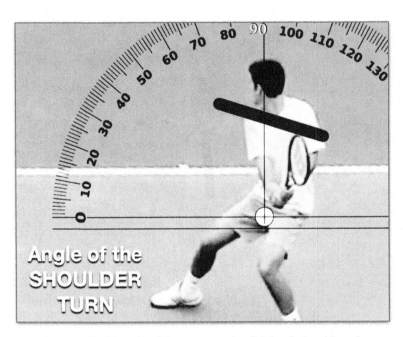

Image 5f. The shoulder turn on the Djokovic backhand.

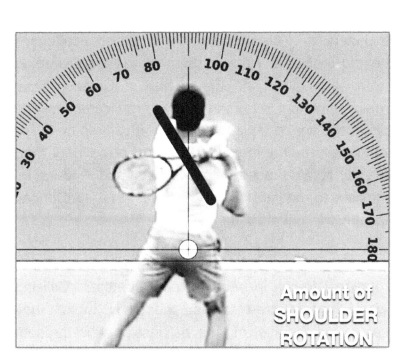

Image 5g. Shoulder rotation on the Djokovic backhand.

The power of rotational forces goes back throughout human history. We are all hardwired to excel at body rotation.

Christopher McDougall's book *Natural Born Heroes* examines a group of people that rediscovered this innate human ability and used it (among other things) to help fight off a pivotal faction of Hitler's army after the onset of the second World War.

The author's inspiration began when he stumbled across the story of Winston Churchill's 'dirty tricksters.' This motley crew of British academics helped resist the Nazi invasion of Crete by learning from each other and the people of Crete. They realized the innate human ability to run incredibly long distances and to replace calories with stored body fat. Aging and outnumbered, this group of ordinary men turned spies tapped into instincts and endurance familiar to ancient Greek cultures that McDougall labeled the lost art of heroism.

The group mastered the explosive strength of rotational forces in hand to hand combat. Utilizing what they referred to as "the body twist," they catapulted themselves into harnessing what present day people would call superhuman strength. The passage below illustrates how body rotation is instinctive, easy to learn, and the strongest move the human body can make.

"The body twist is the basis of all disarming,"
Applegate realized, but that was just the beginning:
for the Twins, the body twist was the basis of
everything. In the jungle, body twist is so potent that
baboons use it as a white flag of surrender; to avoid a
fight, they let their trunk and abdominal muscles sag,
indicating their most powerful weapon has been
deactivated.

Humans, Fairbairn demonstrated, come pre-
equipped with the same primate power. Fairbairn ran

Applegate through a series of gutter-fighting moves— breaking free from a stranglehold; recovering from a knockdown; bringing a bigger man to the ground; and, of course, the "Match-Box Attack."

All Fairbairn's tactics had three things in common: they were quick, easy, and appalling. "Any individual in combat in which his life is at stake very quickly reverts to the animal," it dawned on Applegate. "After a few seconds, and especially after he has been hit or jarred by his opponent, the blood lust is so aroused that from then on his combat is instinctive."

Take the Match-Box. Once you know it, you can walk down a dodgy street at night or escape from gunpoint in the back of a car with nothing more lethal in your pocket than a cell phone—or, in Fairbairn's day, a small cardboard box of matches. If you find yourself in an apprehensive situation, stick close to the walls on the right side of the street and casually slip your right hand into your jacket pocket. Wrap your fist around the phone, with the top just below your thumb and index finger. Damn! You were right to be nervous, because here comes trouble. Someone's moving in fast with—what? a gun? a knife?—in his hand.

The phone will now save your life, but only because of body twist.

"Parry the gun away from your body with your left forearm," Fairbairn instructs. 'Now bring out the phone; by clenching it in your fist, the bones in your hand compress into a hard block.'

Turning your body from the hip, strike your opponent hard on the left side of his face, as near to the jawbone as possible. You barely need to move your arm; keep your shoulder pinned to your side and come up hard with the forearm, letting your hips do the work. "The odds of knocking your opponent unconscious by this method are at least two to one," Fairbairn adds. "The fact that this can be accomplished with a match-box is not well-known, and for this reason is not likely to raise your opponent's suspicion of your movements."

Applegate quickly grasped the power of Fairbairn's discovery. Body twist, like instinctive aim, works for anyone and can be mastered fast: you can pick up the basics in an afternoon and perfect them with just ten minutes or so of daily practice.

You don't need years of training in a dojo and a drawerful of colored belts. What you need most, Applegate realized, is to remember what it's like to fight for real.

Image 5h.

While the benefits of sound shoulder rotation on forehands and two-handed backhands are extensive, the effects are equally problematic when absent. Images 5i and 5j show how the lack of ideal shoulder rotation causes the late impact and stiff-armed, abbreviated finish for WTA Tour pro Sara Errani.   It also shows how former WTA world #1 ranked Ana Ivanovic syncs up her swing path to her ideal shoulder rotation from start to finish, providing her with fluid, effortless power.

Image 5i.

Image 5j.

Image 5k. Del Potro (left) and Djokovic (right).

To simplify ideal shoulder rotation, instructing specific body parts with specific assignments facilitates any technical goal. Because shoulder rotation is the top technical goal, finding ways to fine tune it is paramount.

The tennis gods point specific body parts at the ball at specific moments. Djokovic and Juan Martin Del Potro points their toes at the ball to facilitate ideal shoulder rotation on these backhands in Image 5k. When they step in to load their right legs, they point their right toes at the ball coming.

As they rotate their shoulders through the swing path, their left legs come around to the left side of their bodies. They point their left toes toward the outgoing ball going as they finish.

Image 5l.

In Image 5l, Federer and Djokovic execute ideal shoulder rotation on these forehands by pointing their elbows at the ball. As they load, both men point their left elbows toward the incoming ball to facilitate their approximate 120 degree shoulder turn. As they finish, they point their right elbows at the outgoing ball. This enables the complete rotation of the shoulders and a full, fluid follow through.

Pointing the shoulders at the ball is another great way to enhance both the "shoulder turn" when loading and the "shoulder rotation" when driving through the ball. This serves players as another good option to enable their shoulder turn and rotation while providing some freedom with different body types and personal preferences.

In Image 5n, Stan Wawrinka and Grigor Dmitrov point their left shoulders at the incoming ball as they load. On the follow through they point their right shoulders at the ball they have sent.

Image 5m.

In addition to enhancing fluidity and efficient power generation, executing ideal shoulder rotation gives the tennis gods an easy way to be accurate with their shot making. Backing up serves and returns with accuracy and consistency is a significant factor in how matches are won.

Everyone wants their forehands and two-handed backhands to feel good when they hit them. But don't you want the ball to go where you want it to go even more?

Midway through their nearly 200 degrees of shoulder rotation, Ferrer and Juan Carlos Ferrero make contact with their chests pointing directly toward their intended shot targets in Image 5o below. By facing their targets on impact, they can be confident in their accuracy.

Ferrer's chest points toward his opponent's backhand corner at the moment the ball hits his strings on this inside-out forehand. Ferrero's chest points toward his opponent's forehand corner during impact on this inside-in forehand.

Image 5n.

Of course, this is not the only way to direct the ball. It's just an easy way. Image 5o shows Former ATP #1 ranked Carlos Moya timing the rotation of his shoulders to facilitate shot accuracy.

Image 5o.

Image 5p. The King.

Because all things feed the king, all of the functional training exercises in this book either directly or indirectly promote and enhance shoulder rotation.

Chapter 6. The Supporting Cast

Image 6a.

Anything that influences shoulder rotation must be examined to maximize potential. Aspects of movement ideally serve as a supporting cast for this top priority. The supporting cast includes stances (with the legs) based on the situation, the opposite arm, movement preparation, dynamic balance and momentum.

Executing ideal shoulder rotation becomes easier and more natural when ideal stances are chosen and both arms move relatively together throughout the swing shape. Because of the shot hit from their opponents and the direction they move to receive them, Federer and Murray utilize open stances. Using an open stance and the way they move their left arms in concert with their right arms both facilitate shoulder rotation.

Image 6b.

For players with issues involving the opposite arm on the forehand, functional training is an effective way to problem solve. Images 6c through 6g show functional training solutions for the habit building process of moving both arms on the forehand in concert with one another.

Images 6c and 6d show a medicine ball exercise performed by Clayton Hamilton, one of the pros at our club. Clayton was a former all-conference player in college and now serves as the Head Tennis Coach for Hampton University.

Image 6c.

Holding a football in his right hand to activate his awareness, his objective is to toss me the one pound medicine ball. The toss closely mimics his forehand swing shape, and his task is to hold the football a foot or two ahead of the medicine ball throughout the "stroke."

Image 6d.

This medicine ball exercise was repeated in sets of two or three reps holding a football, he held a red ball, a yellow ball, and even a small kids racquet in his opposite hand to further his awareness. Once we both felt confident in his execution, we did a few reps where he executed a shadow stroke with his racquet while holding one of these balls in his other hand.

This, of course, lead to me hand feeding him some balls where he could hit real forehands (shown in Image 6e) while still holding onto something with his right hand.

Image 6e.

Images 6f and 6g illustrate the next step in this progression.

Image 6f.

Rather than simply holding a medicine ball, or a kid's racquet, or a red, orange or yellow ball in his opposite hand throughout his stroke, Clayton's task this time was to toss or roll whatever he was holding in his right hand to the back curtain during the finish.

Image 6g.

By living through this ten minute progression, which we partially returned to after a short racquet feeding drill and a few live hitting drills, Clayton expressed an increased comfort level regarding his execution of the non-dominant arm on his forehand. His confidence grew further with this skill after we worked through a similar progression during a follow up a few days later.

Image 6h. Lateral Movement of Nikolay Davydenko.

While the use of the non-dominant hand heavily influences shoulder rotation on forehands, dynamic balance and linear momentum dramatically affect shoulder rotation on both forehands and two-handed backhands as well.   While this book's predecessor *How the Tennis Gods Move* explored the connection between linear momentum and dynamic in depth, here we will briefly examine this and look more closely how to train these movement fundamentals.

Maintaining balance on the tennis court is comparable to driving. You drive your car. You press the accelerator and move ahead. If you slam on the brakes, your head and torso would fly forward toward the windshield. Slowing down gradually is easier on your car and your neck. This idea also applies to tennis movement.

Linear momentum is movement in a straight line. For tennis players, this involves moving to set up for the shot as well as moving through the shot (the re-orientation of the feet) during the forward swing. With momentum, using the human body in motion helps the pros generate power, execute ideal shoulder rotation, and maintain dynamic balance. The book *How The Tennis Gods Move* explores these concepts in detail.

In his article for USTA Player Development entitled Movement for Tennis: The Importance of Lateral Training, Mark Kovacs wrote that lateral movement comprises over seventy percent of all shots in tennis.

Images 6i and 6j illustrate a typical example of how Djokovic generates and uses momentum on forehands in this lateral movement situation.

Image 6i. Djokovic's movement preparation

Image 6j. Djokovic's loading and linear momentum.

After moving to his right and loading his right leg, there is a re-orientation of the feet during Djokovic's forward swing. He moves through his shot in the same straight line he ran over to get there. Both feet continue moving to the right during the forward swing and finish.

Moving through the shot takes Djokovic further off the court, which some people might argue is less than ideal. But the benefits heavily outweigh the small cost of being a foot or two further off the court.

Momentum helps Djokovic hit a cleaner shot and recover better. Finishing with his right leg on the outside enables ideal shoulder rotation, which facilitates an ideal contact point and natural finish with the racquet head. It also squares them off to the court for an immediate, balanced recovery.

Images 6k and 6l show how the movement pattern on defensive two-handed backhands executed by Djokovic are nearly identical to what we saw in Images 6i and 6j.

Image 6k.

Image 6l.

102

The ebook version of this book shows videos of top pros in these lateral movement situations like what is illustrated by the Djokovic images above. Over and over, clips of countless pros - many of whom contain different personal styles within their swing shapes - exhibit the same movement patterns that enable them to get to each shot efficiently, load and execute ideal shoulder rotation.

The lateral movement and momentum of the tennis gods can be trained, and below some functional training methods are outlined for players to begin building the same habits.

Taking the racquet out of the exercise can help students focus solely on the movement technique. The shadow exercise shown in Image 6n utilizes two fitness steps. The lateral movement, momentum and rotation are nearly the same on both the forehand and backhand sides.

Variations of one of the functional training exercises already (Image 6m) discussed can be effective in habit forming sound movement fundamentals.

Image 6m. Lateral Movement Functional Training Exercise.

In this exercise, Harrison's task is to begin his movement preparation with his hands in the "pray" position mimic the ready position. His hands execute a shadow stroke as he loads into an open stance on the fitness step and moves through his "shot."

The exercise in Image 6n, like so many others shown in this book, can be done in a variety of ways. The same exercise can be done where the student shadows his stroke with a racquet. Instead of using a racquet and a shadow stroke, a medicine ball toss can also be used.

Image 6n. Lateral Movement Functional Training Exercise.

The fitness step and hoola hoops can serve as interchangeable tools, depending on what the player needs to focus and develop. Image 6o shows Harrison executing the same exercise, but shadowing his stroke with his racquet and loading inside the hoola hoops.

Image 6p also shows the same exercise, but he hops off the fitness step to activate his split step.

Image 6o.

Image 6p.

These exercises also work very well with a medicine ball toss in place of a shadow stroke. Images 6q and 6r illustrate a different combination of the fitness step with the hoola hoops. Harrison's task is to use the fitness step both to load onto and execute a crossover recovery step.

Image 6q.

Image 6r.

As the movement preparation, loading, momentum and shoulder rotation skills develop, eventually players can execute these exercises anywhere on the court and without the fitness step or hoola hoops to guide them, as shown in Image 6s.

Image 6s.

These functional training exercises can easily be done with groups of players too.

Image 6t.

Image 6u.

Chapter 7. The Seven Stages of a Stroke

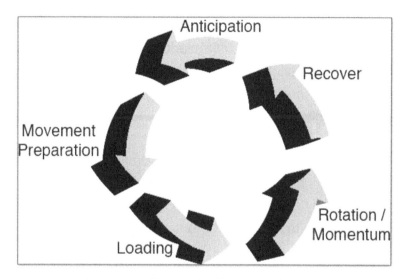

Image 7a. Sequential Movement Patterns

As previously stated, the objective functional training exercises shown in this book is to train sequential movement patterns. Image 7a provides a visual representation of these ideal sequential movement patterns.

The tennis gods use this sequence in conjunction with the timing of their swing shapes. A former USTA coaching colleague Lee Hurst taught me, among other things, the most helpful method of technical analysis I've ever come across.

Hurst's seven stage sequential method brought me out of a fog I had yet to recognize. Tim Mayotte partnered with Hurst to form the Mayotte-Hurst Tennis Academy in New York. Mayotte, a former ATP world #7 ranked American, Wimbledon Semi-Finalist and silver medalist at the 1988 Olympics in Seoul, discussed the seven stages with writer Paul Fein in a recent article for Sport Star Live.

While the BIOMEC Method outlines movement principles, this seven stage sequential method provides a more specific approach to evaluating performance from one shot to the next.

Image 7b. Stages one and two.

"The first stage," Mayotte said, "is the split step for movement and the ready position for the racket. The second stage is the unit turn and the grip change, if needed."

Image 7c. Stages one and two.

"The third stage," said Mayotte, an NCAA singles champion at Stanford, "is the footwork pattern and the racket preparation, also called the take-back." The backswing ideally begins either during or after the shoulders turn further than the hips to activate the loading of the upper body.

Image 7d. Stage three.

Image 7e. Stage three.

Image 7f. Stage four.

"The fourth stage is loading and the racket enters what we call 'the pull position,' which is its path forward."

Image 7g. Stage four.

"The fifth stage," Mayotte continued, "is unloading and the racket goes to contact (the ball)." For forehands and two-handed backhands, this includes the rotation of the shoulders and hips taking place in concert with the start of the foreword swing.

Image 7h. Stage five.

Image 7i. Stage five.

"The sixth stage is when the racket goes to finish and there is a reorientation of the feet." This includes allowing the body in motion to continue moving along the path of linear momentum that the player had to move to prepare for and set up for the shot.

Image 7j. Stage six.

Image 7f. Stage six.

118

Image 7g. Stage seven.

"The seventh stage," Mayotte concluded, "is recovery and back to the ready position."

Image 7g. Stage seven.

Chapter 8. Situational Training

Image 8a.

Most of the time, players at every level during a point will move either laterally, diagonally forward or diagonally backward to prepare for and execute ground-strokes. In a review of pro players' movement entitled *Movement for Tennis: The Importance of Lateral Training*, Mark Kovacs found that more than 70% of movements were side to side.

Image 8b shows the four most common situations right handed players move to hit forehands, while Image 8c shows this for two-handed backhands. Because these situations happen most often during points, players benefit the most from training the seven stages of a stroke in these situations.

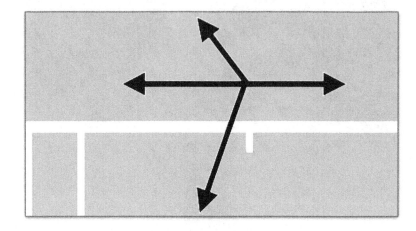

Image 8b.

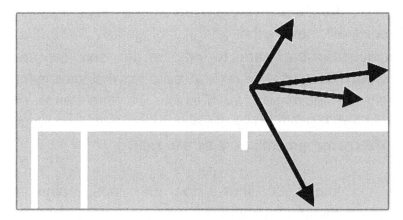

Image 8c.

The images below show some on court progressions used to train lateral movement, momentum and shoulder rotation. Depending on the lesson and the student, the series of exercises shown took between two and ten minutes during the lessons.

Image 8d shows Ashton Legum holding a fitness stick that weights approximately two pounds.

Image 8d.

In this progression, I'm working with Ashton Legum on his lateral movement and shoulder rotation on his forehand. In this first shadow exercise, our tools include the fitness stick and a bosu ball. The fitness stick is useful for helping him pinpoint how much the line of his shoulders turn and rotate.

Ashton's task, shown in image 8e, is to shadow the entire movement, momentum and rotation on a forehand in this lateral movement situation. While holding the fitness stick behind his neck along the line of his shoulders, his task is to initiate a split step, turn and pivot, move to his right and load onto the bosu ball, spring and rotate his shoulders and finish with both feet past the bosu ball.

Image 8e.

After a few reps with the fitness stick, Ashton then performed the same exercise with one difference. This time we used a two pound medicine ball toss (shown in image 8f).

Image 8f.

After a few reps with the medicine ball toss, then we switched the exercise again. Rather than moving and rotating with the fitness stick or tossing me a medicine ball, he executed a shadow swing with his racquet (shown in image 8g).

Image 8g.

Once Ashton did a few reps and we felt confident about his execution of his lateral movement and rotation with his shadow swing, then I hand fed him some real forehands.

Image 8h.

126

Since Ashton had already lived through progressions like this a number of times prior to this lesson, on this particular day, this progression served as a dynamic warm up.

This next example shows a different student, Mya Byrd, going through a quick, simple progression that trains lateral movement and rotation on the forehand. Overall, the progression consisted of (in this order) a medicine ball toss, hand feeding, racquet feeding, and then various types of live hitting.

Image 8i shows the first part of the progression, where Mya executes a medicine ball toss after moving to her right. Images 8j and 8k show Mya moving laterally to hit her forehand in a hand feeding drill.

Image 8i.

Image 8j.

Image 8k.

Lateral and forward movement patterns often include closed stances. Images 8l and 8m show the movement pattern and rotation of the Djokovic two-handed backhand.

Image 8l illustrates the textbook movement fundamentals of Djokovic. His staggered split step is followed by his feet pivoting to his left along with his upper and lower body turning. His center of gravity shifts toward his left prior to a crossover step.

Image 8l.

Image 8m.

130

Djokovic loads his upper body by pointing his right shoulder toward the incoming ball, which allows him to then drop his racquet head into the pull position as he loads his right leg into a closed stance. He rotates his shoulders and hips in sync with the racquet moving through contact. His back left leg moves around to his left on his finish, enhancing the amount of shoulder rotation and squaring him off to the court, which gives him access to an instant recovery.

The following images show functional training concepts to build these fundamentally sound movement habits displayed by Djokovic.

Image 8n.

In the functional training exercise shown in Image 8n, the hoola hoops represent targets that

131

instruct Harrison where and how to move in this shadow stroke. His task is to use the first two hoola hoops to land a split step, and then to make a crossover step into the the third hoola hoop. Then, as he moves toward the ad doubles alley, his final task is to load his right leg into a closed stance in the first of the final two hoola hoops before squaring his body off on the follow through, with his left leg finishing inside the last hoola hoop.

Image 8o.

Images 8o and 8p show a variation of this exercise. Rather than hoola hoops, a fitness step activates Vignesh Akkina's movement preparation.

Image 8p.

As we've previously explored, a medicine ball toss can replace a shadow stroke. In this case (shown in Images 8q, 8r and 8s), the hoola hoops instruct Harrison where to load and finish.

Image 8q.

Image 8r.

Image 8s.

The following images show some functional training progressions during lessons. These images, where students are developing their closed stance backhands, examine how these exercises can work within the context of hand feeding, racquet feeding, live hitting and point play.

Since every player is unique, coaches must explore individually tailored methods of training sound sequential movement fundamentals. Sometimes working backwards is the best way to move forward.

In this case in time, Mya Byrd and I set a performance goal to improve her anticipation. But in observing her movement in point play, her dynamic balance became a question mark at times when she was finishing some of her shots. This made her recovery steps suffer. So it became clear to me that I could not expect Mya to anticipate well when often did not have the time to do so.

The progression below shows how we began to develop this skill. Our first task was to increase her focus on using linear momentum as a tool to develop anticipation.

At this time, Mya Byrd and I worked on her footwork patterns when finishing her shots. Within the sequence of things, we specifically focused on the sixth and seventh stages of her backhand. The sixth stage, "when the racket goes to finish and there is a reorientation of the feet," facilitates dynamic balance. This dynamic balance enhances the seventh stage, which is the recovery.

Mya and I worked on this reorientation of the feet during her finish to enhance her recovery skills. Since our goal was to improve her anticipation, we first had to maximize the amount of time and balance she had to recover after her shots. With more time and balance, she then would have a greater ability to anticipate her opponents' decision making.

The first exercise in the progression (shown in Image 8t) we did was a simple medicine ball toss on her backhand side. We worked on executing all seven stages, highlighting the sixth and seventh stages.

Image 8t.

Mya's task in this progression was to work on the footwork pattern on her closed stance backhand. Specifically, her objective was to move her left foot around to the left side of her body as she tossed me the medicine ball. This squared her off to the court and enabled an immediate recovery.

After a couple sets of a few reps, in the next part in the progression she moved side to side, tossing the medicine ball from closed stances.

Image 8u.

Then we did a few short sets of hand feeding (Image 8v), followed by 1 set of racquet feeding before we did live hitting.

Image 8v.

While some progressions can be simple, others can utilize more functional training tools to develop habits. In the following progression, Ashton Legum and I work on his lateral movement, loading and rotation for his closed stance, two-handed backhand.

While this progression has many similar objectives as the progression Mya Byrd and I conducted, this progression involved adding a few more functional training elements to the process. In this series of exercises, we used a bosu ball, a medicine ball, and a fitness stick prior to hitting any tennis balls.

In the first exercise (shown in Image 8w), Ashton executes a shadow stroke with his racquet, loading his right leg onto the bosu ball.

Image 8w.

For context, while he did few reps of this, we discussed how enhancing the quality of his movement and rotation on his neutral backhand would improve his ability to push his opponents back or wide off the court. This would enable him to use his forehand more often to control the point and increase his net appearances.

Image 8x.

His next task was to perform a full shadow stroke with a fitness stick (shown in Image 8y). We placed a fitness stick behind his neck and along the line of his shoulders (like I'm demonstrating for him in Image 8x).

Image 8y.

After a few reps with the fitness stick, we moved on to a few reps with a medicine ball toss (shown in Image 8z).

Image 8z.

Then we did a small amount of hand feeding to see how well he could reproduce this movement and rotation on a real backhand (images 9a and 9b).

Image 9a.

Image 9b.

One short set of racquet feeding followed (shown in images 9c and 9d), where he had to hit over the teaching basket placed on the other side of the net.

Image 9c.

Image 9d.

Having Ashton hit over the basket was an easy way to maintain the tactical objective of pushing his opponents off the court without us having to talk much about it. This gave me the freedom to continue streamlining my feedback to him about his movement preparation and shoulder rotation.

Prior to point play, Ashton and I progressed through a couple different types of live rallies, where he could transfer the habits he continued to build with the functional training progression.

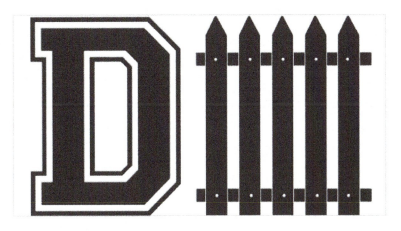

Image 9e. Defense.

With racquet and string technology revolutionizing our sport, players hit shots with more pace and spin than ever before. This puts a player's ability to play effective defense at a premium.

When an opponent sends a heavy, penetrating shot with significant depth during a baseline rally, the tennis gods consistently respond in a similar fashion. They move back, give themselves time, and send a defensive shot with significant net clearance and arc back into the court.

145

My old boss at the Higueras-Gorin Tennis Academy in Sacramento and later at the USTA, taught me a cue word that encapsulates this concept. He called it "absorbing." This worked for me, because verbal shortcuts are meaningful and save time.

The term absorbing refers to the act of moving back to absorb the pace a deep, heavy shot. When executed effectively, absorbing enables the pros to respond to this situation with a smart defensive shot with optimum biomechanics and technique.

Image 9f. Djokovic prepares to absorb a forehand.

Image 9g.

The ideal execution involves using the pace of the incoming ball and backwards linear momentum as sources of dynamic balance, power and time to fully rotate the shoulders throughout the swing path. Djokovic illustrates this in images 9f and 9g.

This, along with aiming for high net clearance and taking pace off the shot, grants the pros greater margin for error in this difficult situation. It gives them more time to recover.

It also increases the chances of sending back a shot with depth, which gives the player a dramatically better chance of preventing his opponent from continuing to attack in the point. Federer shows us this in images 9h and 9i.

Image 9h.

Image 9i.

Andre Agassi illustrates the same concept (images 9i and 9j) with his two-handed backhand.

Image 9i. Agassi preparing to absorb.

148

Image 9j.

Nadal absorbs with similar movement and rotation as well (shown in images 9k and 9l).

Image 9k.

Image 9l.

The images below show students developing their defensive skills with some functional training exercises. To establish trust and get students to buy into the idea of absorbing, I often have them watch a video (which is published in the ebook version of this book) that shows dozens of pros absorbing in the way that Federer, Djokovic, Del Potro and Nadal showed us in the image sequences above.

Darby Hunt begins this progression with a functional training exercise (shown in images 9m and 9n) where she executes a shadow stroke, loading onto a bosu ball.

Image 9m. Shadow stroke with a bosu ball.

Image 9n.

After this particular rep, the coaching feedback I gave was that she had a nice wide base when loading and good overall shoulder rotation, but that on the next few reps she should keep the line of her shoulders (posture) and upper body more level (no leaning).

After a few reps with the shadow stroke, we moved on to a medicine ball toss (images 9o and 9p). This improved in the next step in the progression, which was a medicine ball toss.

Image 9o. Medicine ball toss with a bosu ball.

Image 9p.

By the time we began some hand feeding, the functional training exercises had helped Darby establish more of a comfort level with the movement and rotation when absorbing on defense.

Image 9q.

Image 9r.

Darby later expressed that the development of these defensive skills enhanced her belief that she could play at a higher level. She felt that, because she was confident in her ability to handle difficult situations in rallies, she would be able to stay in rallies that previously she could not.

She also expressed confidence in her ability to neutralize her opponents' best shots, reset rallies, and subsequently control points more often. This proved true, because she knew the movement, mechanics, and shot selection to respond in these scenarios.

Conclusion

Image 8a.

"You get the game to do the teaching for you!" Judy Murray said at a coaches conference I attended many moons ago.

Mike Barrell (founder of Evolve 9) echoed that sentiment at another presentation I observed. "If the game is structured well, players can learn without the coaches preaching at them."

Drills and exercises can also serve this function for skill acquisition. In a well-designed drill or exercise, players can build habits with sound fundamentals without the coaches constantly preaching at them.

People learn by seeing and doing and understanding. Some learn better through auditory listening, others learn by seeing and mimicking, and others still learn more kinesthetically.

Most tennis players learn best when they experience a combination of the three. The functional training concepts shown throughout this book provide players with all of these things.

Players can refine their biomechanics in a profound, lasting way because the functional training exercises add visual and kinesthetic elements that boost mind body awareness. They help build fundamentally sound habits faster and more effectively than just by listening to feedback and hitting a ton of balls.

As we see from top pros in this book, great movement fundamentals enable great confidence. It enables the pros to maximize the amount of time to hit each shot, which dramatically affects how well they strike the ball from one shot to the next. It significantly expands tactical options within a point and allows them greater access to implementing various strategies within matches.

Great movement fundamentals enable players to maximize their efficiency, which over the course of a match allows players to operate with enhanced endurance.   An efficient mover saves energy compared to an inefficient mover.

A fresh player will be more likely than a tired player to perform with positive energy. This increases that player's likelihood of starting matches off with poise. A physically fresh player is also more likely to retain focus deep in a third or fourth or even fifth set.

The quality of a player's footwork on the tennis court is affected by that player's foot speed. However, the effectiveness of a player's overall movement has much more to do with the habits built over time with *how* they move to and from each shot.

These exercises can serve a variety of purposes. One such purpose could be, for example, as a way for coaches and players to discover the movement habits in various situations - or lack thereof.

I find that having players execute shadow strokes with their racquet of the 4 most common forehands or backhands, for example, can be very revealing. It can illuminate to the player and coach where the players habits and knowledge base resides at that moment.

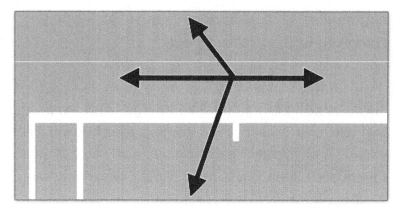

Image 8b.

In image 8c, Darby executes the first 2 shadow strokes of the 4 most common forehands. After 1 rep of moving to her right, she does 1 rep moving to her left for an inside out forehand.

Image 8c.

Her 3rd and 4th reps are shown in image 8d, where she moves diagonally forward for a short ball and diagonally back to absorb a deep ball.

Image 8d.

Throughout these shadow exercises, isolated skills like the split step, shoulder rotation, arm extension, cross over steps, and many other technical aspects can become the spotlight to which player and coach focus. Primary objectives in these exercises, depending on player specific needs, can be anything.

On this particular day for Darby, the quality of her finish served as our focus. We both paid attention to the sixth stage of her stroke. So as she followed through on each shadow stroke forehand, my comments reflected what I saw regarding the reorientation of her feet during her follow through and how well she finished the rotation of her shoulders.

Because there is no possibility of making or mission a shot in these shadow exercises, players can become fully immersed in the improvement task at hand. Even in the case where movement fundamentals are not the primary focus, players can concentrate on a specific technical aspect of their stroke while building subconscious habits.

For Harrison Lee, this relentless immersion in the task at hand helped him not only develop sound movement habits in these common forehand situations, it also enabled him to develop mental skills on the court. An enhanced understanding of his own mechanics grew his self reliance. It enabled his ability to problem solve and coach himself during matches. These factors lead to an ongoing discussion about his development of a growth mindset.

Over time, Harrison became fluent in these exercises. This enabled us to transition these functional training exercises, taking them out of the skill development progressions during our lessons and insert them into dynamic warm ups - like the one shown in images 8e, 8f and 8g.

Image 8e.

Image 8f.

Image 8g.

With a dynamic warm up like this one, Harrison has the habits of his movement and rotation fundamentals reinforced. This helps stabilize his racquet head technique, boosts his knowledge of ideal mechanics, self reliance and self confidence.

About the Author

Daniel McCain is the author of other critically acclaimed books, including *Building a Champion*, *The I Formation*, *Momentum*, and *How the Tennis Gods Move*. He was named the 2012 USTA Virginia Teaching Pro of the Year, the 2013 PTR Mid-Atlantic Teaching Pro of the Year, and the 2014 PTR Virginia Member of the Year.

McCain has been published in Tennis Life Magazine, PTR Tennis Pro Magazine, Tennis View Magazine, Tennis One, USTA Player Development website, TennisPlayer.net, Elite Tennis (GPTCA publication), and MomentumTennis.com.

McCain currently resides in Virginia Beach, Virginia and serves the Cavalier Golf and Yacht Club as the Director of Tennis. He serves the Professional Tennis Registry (PTR) as a Clinician and Tester, running coaches workshops across the United States. He also serves Universal Tennis as a UTR Ambassador

A Graduate of the ITF Junior Tennis School, McCain is an ATP Certified Coach through the GPTCA, a USTA High Performance Certified Coach, and a PTR Professional. He also achieved certifications in technique through Vic Braden's Tennis College and as an ITPA Tennis Performance Trainer from the International Tennis Performance Association.

A former USTA Manager of Player Development and NCAA Division 1 College Coach for 7 years, McCain was the Director of Tennis at The Higueras-Gorin Tennis Academy, served as a USTA National Team Coach in 2015, and coached for Team USA in 2015 and 2016.

As a player, McCain achieved a junior ITF world ranking and won both gold and silver balls, winning the USTA National Indoor championship and reaching the finals of the USTA National Clay Courts. He played for the University of Michigan tennis team on scholarship where he finished his undergraduate degree with concentrations in Journalism and Psychology.

McCain then completed post graduate work from Illinois State University, with a concentration in graphic design. He also studied at the American Board of Sport Psychology in a masters level program focusing on performance psychology and critical moments in competition.

www.DanMcCain.com